Parkinso
'One More Sleep'
By
Philip B. Gibbs

Explanation

I have been asked to comment on how I arrived at some of the more unnatural ways of expressing myself in verse.
Some of it is due to the influence of 'homework' for college and some is directly due to me, trying out various layouts and forms of verse which are different. The real heart of the poems is to try to capture the nature of Parkinson's Disease and its changeable effect on individuals.
Everyone is different.

This is my story

Not always in the right order, but truthful none the less.
Parkinson's is a nasty disease which induces all sorts of mind changing episodes. Ridiculous dreams like 'White Van Man' and beneficial dreams like 'The Rain Man' or 'The Sea I See' become mixed up with the pugilistic input of my brain in lashing out at whatever or whoever is in my dream with me at the time! Parkinson's – you are a nasty, nasty disease. I am not a fighter or a rough natured person usually but the personality changes which Parkinson's puts upon you are very upsetting at times.

Still I have to live with it, as do lots of other people and this little book will go some way to allowing me to let off steam – in the nicest possible way!

An Authors OnLine Book

British Library Cataloguing Publication Data.
A catalogue record for this book is available from the British Library

ISBN 978-0-7552-1611-6

Authors OnLine Ltd
19 The Cinques
Gamlingay, Sandy
Bedfordshire SG19 3NU
England

This book is also available in e-book format, details of which are available at www.authorsonline.co.uk

ii

Foreword

All my life I have had a feeling that anything anybody else can do, I can do also. Maybe not as well, but I can do it. All it takes is application : be it brain surgery, painting and decorating, sweeping the roads, or writing books (either novels or poetry.)

Having taken a short course at the local College, I collected together all my draft paperwork, decided to go to a publisher, and try my luck. The very next day I received an e-mail from my lecturer saying that she was about to create a publishing house, to which I replied – 'Count me in!' There is nothing like the thrill of being in the vanguard of a new enterprise (an hour and a half after its launch!) although that hasn't come about, I trust that is how you will feel with this new venture on my part.

My thanks go to Amanda–Jane for her stimulation and encouragement, and to you, for purchasing what is obviously an effort well worth your participating in.
Read on kind friend,

and

Welcome.

Acknowledgement

To : D.I.Rudd Esq. My Friend.

My sincere thanks go to 'my friend' (that was) who became bemused by hy-phens, dots, colons, and inverted commas in the original text but in true British style and English teacher fashion, proof read this script to a conclusion.

Thank you David, for your hours of leisure spent reading this and trying to decipher it. For your gentlemanly remonstrations with me. (The author both of your mental tiredness and your lost leisure time.)

My thanks go also to my Love's Farm Community Association Committee who lost out in performance on my part, during the typing at snail's pace of this document. A huge project to undertake on my own.

Love and Best Wishes to my wife and family who had no small part in creating this me, who then sat down and wrote these poems - easily.

Go safely with your Lord,
Philip B. Gibbs

In the next paragraph you will see Parkinson's at work. David Rudd was a normal Secondary School teacher who loves the English Language and is sorry that I do not follow the rules.

My Rules are easy.

Write it how you like. So long as it is clear and intelligable.

David Rudd wrote:

I picture you sitting in your embroidered cap and embroidered smoking jacket. Ready to write a poem. You sit before your table, six neatly sharpened quills near your right hand, with your ink newly stirred at the top right-hand of your parchment. You flex your fingers, then you warm them at the candle flame which burns at the back of the table.

You pick up a quill, but then you put it down again. Forgotten something?

Gotcha!! Now I know your little secret. Yes! I have found you out! I have worked it out. Your secret is open for all the world to see!

You pick up a little pepper pot which is filled with 'Fairy Dust' of parentheses and hyphens and before you start to write you sprinkle a few onto the the new clean parchment - and you are off!!

'Gotcha'!

So, my secret is out.

I have to confess that I need to find my pepper pot and 'Have a sprinkle'! before David has a turn and is put away for a long sentence. (There are plenty of those in the following pages.)

I hope that you enjoy finding them where-ever they occur.
Philip B. Gibbs.
June 2nd 2014.

Contents

Contents (contd.)

Parkinson's and Me

There is one thing that you should know
I've found my Parkinson's a blow.
Still I cannot take it seriously
Although my death it will oversee.
It hasn't got the strength to kill
And yet it makes a body ill
Enough to let some other germ
Into the system to do the harm.

So why is it that I don't care
When my friends can't help but stand and stare
At shaking hands and eyes that glare
And a mouth that dribbles in the air?
You see, they cannot see inside
The way my heart just swells with pride
When I manage to do something denied
Like put on socks or my tie I've tied.

It is the little things in life,
Like my new Jenny (she's my wife).
At five foot nothing – not too tall,
But a brilliant organiser overall.
She arranges things, where're she goes
And keeps most people on their toes.
Why have I bothered to mention this?
It's because to her I am a 'miss'.

I take no notice, go my way
Although I know I'll rue the day
When some cruel circumstance will say
'I told you 'No!', there's Hell to pay!'
And this is where I first came in
With careless pose and upward chin.
Some of my poems are 'Black as Sin'
But please read on, you may even grin!

That was the Introduction, now to the 'real stuff.'

Modern Poetry and Me

I've joined the class, for good or ill,
For many a friend would call out – 'Phil.
Write me a line or two in verse
As my iambic's getting worse!'

To keep a rhythm really is a whim
Of mine, first noted in the hymn
Which I had sung (and sung) at school;
It locked my brain into its chanting rule.

How hard it is to break out from its hold,
But I will do it, so I have been told.
Not in this verse, for this one's set to rhyme.
I'll just compose it all some other time.

I'll take a theme, like, 'What did someone say?'
Which locked into my brain on that sad day.
Forget iambics, rhythm and the rhyme,
Forget the 'Good Old Rules', forget the time

When poets heeded Shakespeare's golden rule
Of fourteen lines, which rhymed, and was the pull
For Wordsworth's sonnets, which may not be read
Unless I take this booklet up to bed.

I think poetic discipline has gone.
Yet it is this which really spurs me on
To have a try at writing without rules,
Because it's modern and it's done in schools.

So, wait awhile, be patient, take a rest –
A poem's coming on. Could be my best!

That sad day' -
'What did he say?'

The river, black and cold, runs deep.
Its bank confused with reeds is steep.
It's one o'clock in the morning,
Four hours 'til dawning.
The helicopter's loud hovering
Cracks the night.
A million watts of searchlight
Blinking on and off
Illuminating all things in its Spartan circle
Of steel cold light –
Into which I am drawn.

Heat sensors search the reeds, my dog
Is blinded by the intensity of light.
A policeman appears suddenly, out of the dark.
'Have you seen anyone?' I thought he asked.
'Not a soul' I stiffly remarked.
A search is on
Into which I am drawn.

The elderly lady meanders, lost, frightened, bemused.
A teacher of children, yet still utterly confused
By Ofsted's needs and stultifying rules,
She cannot cope in satisfying all those fools.
Decision made, note written, death resolved
She is on her own, no-one else involved.

How will it feel, the water in her nose,
The cloying weight of water-sodden clothes,
The filling lungs, the lack of air
The glazing eyes which only stare?
Too late the search
Into which I am drawn.

How can a job of work cause
So much pain, that life
Is nothing and so quickly gone?
'What did he say, boy?' I ask the dog.
And so starts years of talk, about
'The worth of work' –
Into which I am drawn.

Work – something different!

I sit here tired and quite frustrated,
Book-keeping (as a job), is overrated.
Nothing I touch, is in its place,
I don't look good with egg on my face.

I promised the accountant (who's really a friend),
That I would be ready by January end.
The Reason for that is easily told,
There's a £100 fine to 'come in from the cold'

So, I've got to get going, to sort out this mess,
I can't find the records of payments. No less.
I did have them once. So, where are they now?
They have all reached the shredder, been shredded:
and How!!

I bought one of those shredders which cut it both ways.
Don't know how it does it, but one of these days
I'll take it to pieces (for which I'm renowned)
And have all its inner parts, left lying around.

I must stop this divergence at once; can you see
What a lovely distraction it is proving to be?
I've not checked one new figure, for nearly an hour
And all my good humour is now turning sour.

It is turning against me, because of my mistake
In thinking I'd remember the deposits I'd make.
There is no way with Parkinson's disease of the brain
That things you've forgotten will re-appear again.

They are gone for all time, there is nowhere else to look
So I'll shut down the computer, and then close the book
The one that is giving me the greatest form of trouble
'Cos I've done it 'Single Entry', instead of doing 'Double.'

I've tried my very hardest to make sense of this account
To avoid the big fine which the Taxman will mount
On the thirty-first of January two thousand and twelve.
He will first start by fining me and then start to delve.

Once he starts delving he'll soon realise,
That I put in my own money. I'm telling no lies.
So I'd like to get it out again for spending on me
And I'll close down the company, albeit happily.

{A slight change (in gender!) }
I 'found' these words.............

I found these words at the back of a drawer
All neatly written in script.
They tell of the life of a woman called Shawyer
Just before she entered the crypt.

It tells of her childhood, the beatings at school
When recital of verses went wrong.
How with sore hands and bruised legs, she'd sit on her stool,
Yet her heart would still break into song.

Her teenage was short–lived, because she could write
And read and do sums and such things,
So she soon became needed by all on the site
Of her father's inventions – like 'Springs'.

He invented a method of 'case – hardening' steel,
Which invited young men to the place.
One of them stole her heart and made her feel
As though she'd explode in his face.

Her love was returned, but no further pursued,
For bankruptcy came on the scene
And a life of domestic appointments ensued,
With abuse and vile treatment obscene.

These words were the record of a woman in strife,
Of changes which really appal,
They highlight the trauma of how she lived life,

WHEN I WROTE THEM I CANNOT RECALL.

Where has Love Gone?

I am just sixteen, gauche and rarey,
Find all girls both strange and scarey
In my head.
All my body functions grapple,
Feeling love grow - how to tackle
In my head
'Where has love gone?'

Met my wife, who changed my life
Gave me children without strife
In my head.
Love died quickly, once we lost them
To their other halves – and then
In my head
'Where has love gone?'

It's gone for ever. All the passion,
All the fire and warmth I fashion
In my head.
Then I make a new decision
To move out – and make division
In my head.
Where has love gone?

Twenty years I chase, pursue love
Thinking I can rise above
In my head.
Then I found my feet were pinned down
By a friend who's earned a crown
In my head.
'I know just where love has gone!'

It's gone inside, rekindling passion
In my heart. In modern fashion
In my head.
Love grew quickly, all enfolding
Makes me hasten to proposing.
In my head
'I know just where love is found.'

It is found in this relationship –
Cures the hurt of broken kinship
In my head.
Brings fulfilment, satisfaction
In checking, valuing every action
In my head.
'I now know that I have found love!'

Seven Decades -
Three score years and ten

Three score and ten, my mother said
Was in the bible so she'd read.
It's just the length of life which each
Of God's new children is to reach.

I reached this earth in Thirty-nine
As baby new – I was DIVINE!!
I cried three months; my brother said
'Just send him back – or he'll be dead!'

At age of **TEN** - my first decade,
I went to choir school, all fees paid.
I'd sung in choirs since age of five,
At Boarding School I just survive!

At **Twenty** I got married – when
A child arrived right there and then!
Just look at this; four very young ones
And all that due to – Pickled Onions.?

By **Thirty**, three decades have gone
And business presses on and on.
Family life begins to suffer
And I don't notice – what a duffer.

Forty – half of life has passed,
How do I feel? Well no–one asked,
Yet rubbish statements I seem to utter
And my memory begins to stutter.

Fifty – Habits change to 'Sloane',
Have left the wife, and live alone.
Hate dusting, washing up, and ironing.
Love freedom, trips – try 'anything'!

At **Sixty**, I have 'Secret' party,
Everyone is Hale and Hearty
Eating 'Chinese' by the plateful,
I make jokes and choke on mouthful!

Seventy is dawning fast
Life and I are near our last.
What you don't know – even yet
Is Parkinson's made me forget.

Parkinson's – that nuisance plot
In my life the only 'Blot'.
I will eradicate its message
And ignore its creeping passage.

TEN DECADES is my intent,
The Bible's span I do resent.
Life is too good to give away
I'll live it by one day-to-day.

TEN DECADES – Am I being greedy?
I'll use the time to help the needy.
My recollections all seem sad
So I'll use the time to make me glad.

That **Gladness** I will surely store,
'Cos older memories are no more.
This **Writing** is the **right** incentive
'Damn' – pen's run out – **Excuse invective!.**

MY (White Van Man.) DREAM

I've never made love in the back of a van,
Yet one young lady tells me, "If I'm gentle, I can!!"
She mentioned a layby, but didn't say where
So I don't know if I'm to take her or just meet her there.

To a gent such as me, it doesn't seem quite right,
To expect a young lady to arrive late at night.
So I'll arrange to collect her, I'll knock at the door
And if her husband answers I'll tell him the score.

This offer to return me to the days of my youth,
Was too good to miss, (now I'm long in the tooth,)
I can't sit for too long, and my back is quite bad,
So as a CV for making love, its reading is sad.

How can I clamber up into the back once more,
Of my white "Passion Wagon" with mattress on the floor
And large white plastic packing cases stacked door to door,
Taking up the very space for which I explore?

So very regrettably there is nothing doing,
I can cope, just so long as there is no wooing.
Your husband can forget his expensive suing
Because it's all in a dream, there is nothing brewing.

I've been stopped in this layby now for over one whole hour
The air is turning blue, and my mood is turning sour,
The snow is drifting up the glass, I'm becoming very cold,
I've run out of my driving hours, I must be getting old.

I'm sat here in the drift of sleep, not one thing or the other.
If I don't make a move soon, don't think I'll need to bother,
For I was told, before I left , that I had a little list
Of all the things that yesterday, in Tesco's I had missed.

I have my present for my wife, here, in the van with me
And, if I don't get it home on time, I think that I could be
A statistic in the paper and it won't be on page three –
But tucked up in the murders, even though she's ninety-three.

It is strange that when you've done your three score years and ten,
You seem to all start cracking up and for your pills you yen.
You suffer with these strange wild dreams, like I did, just before
A policeman came and woke me up by knocking on the door.

The Mirror

Mirror – you reflect the light
Making daylight of the night,
Making my reflection bright.
Is that me? That awe full sight?

Mirror – I am full of doubt
As to what I am about.
Is this swelling due to gout?
Or nothing more than a splash of grout?

Mirror – must you show the fault
Which my friends have said means nought?
Yet to me brings moods, distraught,
Depressive even, sad and fraught.

Mirror – You return my stare
Is that really me that's there
With my 'being' all laid bare?
And you without a trembling care.

Mirror - You have much to answer,
For you see I'm just a 'chancer'
'Chanced' to see my 'SELF' was ever
Growing older 'everywhere'!

Mirror - full length – circle – square,
I guess your're smirking hanging there,
Upsetting those who have to stare,
Those who like me, take no real care.

Mirror – Wait, things aren't so bad
Morning's coming – makes me glad;
Glad to be alive – not sad
With all the active life I've had.

Mirror – Daylight's here at last
And the hell of night has passed.
Things look rosey, I move fast
To dress, and eat a fine repast.

Mirror – I'm flattered when I see
My reflection, my 'new' me.
Crisp white shirt, new tie, trilby.
A 'dapper gent!' – What mystery?

Mirror - the 'Mystery' is this –
One thing is certain – that's Death's kiss.
Like you who bid the night – 'Resist'.
I shall die happy, full of bliss.

Mirror – you show me all my faults.
Teach me to accept them (with the warts).
Turn them to good, by pleasant thought
I'll live life blessed – not sad and fraught.

HAND in HAND

(A Poem written by the Chairperson from the perspective of a
guest at The Parkinson's Society's Branch Lunch – April 2008.)

I opened up the hotel door
And wondered what I'd come here for.
Lots of people I do not know!
All with PD? That is so.

Here I am, a guest at dinner,
They call it Lunch, now that's a winner!
I feel for the chap who is in the Chair -
The one place I wouldn't sit, is there.

He rushes round, greets all and sundry,
Talks to both Mayors, converses brightly.
Yet I can see he is wound up tight
It will take some time to unwind tonight.

He checks his watch, it's just on one
He bangs his gavel, sounds like a gun.
'Please take your seats. I will say Grace,'
Poor fellow's scared, it's in his face.

He starts and falters. What's the matter?
Forgot the mike, the sound is better,
He says his words, an unusual grace,
It puts a smile upon every face.

We are now expecting to eat our lunch
When the air is cut by an awful crunch.
It's that gavel again, just rending the air
We welcome the speaker the guests who are there.

We then eat our lunch, very good (as it goes),
Young chicken in sauce, and profiteroles.
As coffee is served, the Gavel goes crack –
A ten minute 'comfort' break, 'Don't be late back!'

He now makes his speech to introduce Vinny,
And leaves her a problem, which isn't too funny.
He ended his speech with a bit of a joke
Saying, 'Think on this statement - which somebody spoke.

The brain starts to work at the moment of birth,
But stops at the instant' (this said without mirth),
When asked to speak publicly at an event.
My brain has now 'stopped', as is quite evident!'

What a frightful introduction, but our speaker is good,
She has thought on her feet, as up she stood.
'Hope my brain's not dead yet, 'cos I've plenty to say
In just twenty minutes, not like you, the whole day!'

There were plenty of figures, facts and some fun,
The overall feeling was – Very well done.
A sincere vote of thanks, presentation of flowers.
Good Lord, do you realise we've sat here three hours!

I have sat as a guest, noting all I have seen,
There are some things I'd change, if in charge I had been.
Overall I enjoyed it, I now understand
How a 'Chairperson' works – It's with us *Hand in Hand.*

Poem Written Short

Have I written words on politics before?
Not sure.
Here I lay my case at Brown's front door
For sure.

Nobody asked him to take up the reins of power
And as for it being settled prior
To labour's winning a landslide overall majority, it
Led to a misleading of the public on a grand scale for
We the punters knew nothing of this fix.
Had it been known that we were voting for a 'Browned-
off Blair'

Half the vote would not be there.
The nasty bastard (apologies to his Dad),
Took 5 billion out of my pocket
And **prudently** reduced my Pension by a third, without so
much as a 'by your leave'.

Every statement made by him, is led into by the big word 'I'
'I have decided the country needs…'
'I have been **prudent** in arranging to….'
'I have taken back my 10p tax band'
'I know best - you're safe in my hand!'
The man's a Scot, a canny lot,
And so are most of the government.
This devolution heaven sent - to represent
With Scots - the English Parliament.
The Low or Highland twang cuts like a knife
As they sort out our melancholy form of life,

High taxes, bills and petrol too
Where will it end? I'm asking you.
Where will this Scottish Premier lead us?
What will he do to help and feed us?
The great 'I am' has disappeared
In clouds of indecision,
Now that power has engulfed him
Maybe the end.....!
Will come in an Election!

Verse 2 :

I've written my thoughts on Brown
Down.
I now add what I think, on
Cameron.
…...
…...
…………………………………
…………………………………
That is **that** said, sweet and short
Enough said – it's a **FULL** report.

Verse 3 :

As for the Liberal Dems
Them's
Without names of any sort!

I'm feeling better!

I've read 'Recovered' by Ros Barber.
Wish I hadn't – 'cos it's harder
To understand my complex plight
Of writing poems in the night.

I was depressed, or so I thought.
Now all my thinking, counts for naught.
'You're looking so much better now'
My friends all say – but when, or how?

Did they decide a concerted plot
Would override my decision not
To let this misery fade away
Or last for just one extra day?

'Cheer up! Old lad, it's not so bad,
Your old pal David lost his dad,
His mother too in double quick time,
His sister's ill and in her prime.'

I take this in – I justify
The reason I just thought I'd die,
I look at myself, there's nothing wrong,
There's just something for which I long.

The trouble is I can't decide
Upon the thing from which I hide.
This indecision shows its place
Within my thinking – on my face.

It's this that all my friends could see
And why they really angered me.
Why can't they just leave well alone
And greet me with a joyful tone?

Well here we go! I'm off again,
Can it be me – slightly insane?
Upset by greetings and by letter
'Why Phillip, must say you're looking better!'

Better than what, or when, or how?
How do I really look right now?
Shall I be confined this coming night
To writing poems – without light?

'Full circle' – I have gone around
Been over all this very ground
Not once, not twice, a million times
It all ends up in some written lines.

These lines pour forth with random ease,
No thought is given, if you please
To what effect there just might be
If I looked better, when you last saw me!

Then you would say something like 'Phil,
Since we last met, you do look ill.'
Immediately, I'd understand
And put 'recovery' in hand.

And suddenly, my life would change,
And everything would be in range
And I'd become a real 'go getter'
Because right now **I'm feeling better!**

Something Novel
(The PD need to use the Toilet at night)

It is half past twelve in the morning
My body awakes without warning.
I lie here awaiting the dawning
And try hard - to avoid my loud yawning.

What reason can my body have
To wake me? I don't need the Lav,
In any case I'd need Sat Nav
To locate the Loo, that I have.

In my younger days, I did not think –
So it caused my sleep pattern, to shrink
Whilst locating the toilet, I'd blink
And into the Wardrobe I'd slink.

I had a successful need
To join that illustrious breed
Of men boasting loudly – 'I've peed'.
While their wives say – 'Oh have you, indeed?

Then you'd best get yourself out of bed,
Take deep breaths as you clear your thick head.
My new costume's the one coloured red,
If it's damaged my boy, then you're dead!'

All this started 'cos I'm taken short,
A new costume (in red) I have bought!.
A new wardrobe's as likely as nought.
And could have been avoided – with thought!

So, what did the Consultant say
When we met at his clinic to-day?
'I hear your nighttime's gone astray-
Well I've tablets to fix that to-day!'

So out he comes with some pills
Which are guaranteed to end my ills.
They dry 'everything' up with no frills
And the box says – 'These tablets are Phil's'

I now look about eightythree,
I used to have 'water on the knee',
From this hospital bed I can see
Lack of liquids is 'doing' for me.

It is half past twelve in the morning
My body awakes – without warning.
I lie here awaiting the dawning
And try hard - to avoid my loud yawning.

What reason can my body have
To wake me? I don't need the Lav,
In any case I'd need Sat Nav
To locate the Loo, that 'THEY' have.

Being Alive

The diagnosis

I walk tall to the hospital door.
I ask the way – Oh what a bore,
A half mile walk, stairs, second floor
Clinic 12, name on the door.
It's Dr. Lennox in attendance
My thanks for that. 'Cos with a vengeance
I can tell him things which simply
Are the truth (however grimly).
He states the facts, my flesh goes pimply!
'It's Parkinson's'. I hear it – **Limply.**

Living with it

I knew nothing. To me it is perfectly clear
Of Parkinson's hurtfulness and raw-boned fear.
Fear generated by lack of emotion.
Falling down, getting up, what a commotion.
Insidious happenings, tremors and drooling,
Freezing and stiffness, these symptoms aren't fooling.
The **'LIFE – SPARK'**, rekindled by friends and relations
Consultants and Research in so many nations,
They are all there to help me, so why should I care
When my love of life will beat every despair?

Dealing with Hallucinations

I lie in bed at dark of night,
so full of joy at what's gone right
I coped with argument and stress
with kissing, laughter, forgetfulness.

What fun I had with my love Jenny.
Some holds barred? There just aren't any!
So, why is it in the depth of sleep
I suddenly awake and keep -

On seeing things that are not there?
Why do I lie and sweat and stare?
Why does the light move round and shatter
and all my good intentions scatter?

I must get up, but I'm too afraid.
Perhaps I'd best employ an 'aid'.
Friends would think it was not in keeping
when all I need is a manual for sleeping

Which would explain the 'noises off';
was that a footfall or a cough?
'Oh Doctor, help me beat this thing'.
Oh telephone – Why don't you ring?

The 'B(L)ACKSIDE OF PARKINSON'S'
What you get for not taking your tablets on time

Explanation : In all the time I have been coming to see our Parkinson's Specialist Nurses at their clinics I have been 'economical with the truth'. There is a reason for this, and it is, that up to now I have always had my day's quota of tablets, if not in the right order. But order is the wrong definition for PD.
It is imperative to have the bulk of the medication on time at the agreed time,
in order to treat your symptoms properly!!

So,

Whenever I sat down and wrote
A poem, which I thought of note,
I soon discovered to my loss
I really couldn't give a toss.
Each verse's content would declare
Some garbled truth beyond compare,
With which I'd wrestled night and day
And dealt with in my own sweet way.

'What garbled truth?', I hear you say,
As I confess to another day
When tablet taking should – by rote,
Be something over which I gloat!.
But yet, it's eight years to the day
Since all these tablets came my way,
And still I cannot train my brain
To take them, to avoid the pain.

You see, I know I'm doing wrong
When my watch keeps going 'BONG'
And I have got no pills to take.
What's wrong with me for heaven's sake?
My PD Nurse has oft' explained
How taking pills needs to be trained.
Nine when I rise, three more at lunch,
Five after tea creates the 'crunch'!

A hundred times it's been explained
Until my nurse is nearly drained
Of all emotion, love and care
But still she keeps on trying, where
A lot would soon have given in,
My cussedness is like a sin.
I feel it coming, (it's justified!),
She aims a kick at my 'Backside!'

OUCH !! That smarts!!

Electronic Golf.

Explanation: This poem is just to prove that not everything I write is to do with Parkinson's. This certainly isn't! Though it has come to light since this was written that a Wii machine can have very beneficial effects for PD sufferers, both in balance, timing, exercise and screaming!

She's playing with my Wii,
It's golf- so they tell me,
 'Get it in the hole in three'
Or scream quite viciously.

She screamed and screamed out loud,
She'd missed – It's in the crowd.
A 'drop shot' now is needed
To continue – so she pleaded.
The rest is history.
The game's a mystery.
Her brother swings the sticks so well
She tells him he can go to............make a cup of tea!!

A Parkinson's Day 'Trip'
(Usually taken at night, while asleep)

I'm feeling well,
Walked to the dell,
Slipped and fell,
Rolled pell-mell.
'Hell.'

Shoe lost grip,
Made me slip.
Broke a leg
Just like egg
Shell.

Knocked out cold.
Grew old
quickly; voices said
At my head –
'Swell.'

Did I die?
'No!': I lie.
Then I burned,
Tossed and turned.
'Well?'!

Now it's nice
to have paid the price.
Heavenward bound,
Listen to the sound
Gel.

Angels sing.
Everything
has the ring
for bettering
Hell!

The Blackbird's Song

Oh ! Heavenly sound that I recall
Of clear sweet notes with no repeats
And as I listen I grow tall
Drawn up to where that great heart beats.

The Thrush, whether speckled, brown or song
Or even Mistle needs careful and long
Searching in places hidden away
Making life live for another day.

The thrush is repetitive, the Blackbird is not
The Thrush sings its chorus as if a 'job lot'.
The Blackbird has whistles and trills, some sublime,
Dear Lord may this lovely bird exist for all time.

Depression versus 'Love of LIFE'.

It's Death who stares at me across the room
And he has done so, since my mother's womb
Released me into this, my lifelong tomb
And taught me how to play the sombre tune
Required by life and everything that lives,
Which means it often takes and sometimes gives
To those whose life is lessened by demand
Of circumstances dread, with no command.
And yet, I see right now, a 'rosy hue',
Because I met and fell for one like you
Whose 'neat-and-tidy' habits get things done,
Whose love surrounds and wraps up everyone.
Oh would that I could also be the same
And **'love of life'** for once and all reclaim.

The Rainman

'You're dying tonight' said the man made of rain,
As my life flashed by on the wall again.
Everything I had been was recalled for sure
And my God stood alone by an open door.

I knew it was He, for the brilliant light
Made the daytime I was in, seem like the night.
The sun became dark, the atmosphere heavy
As my body recoiled from paying life's levy.

Most people wonder if there's any pain hereafter.
I can explain that it's memories and laughter
Fill in the passing time, (which doesn't exist),
There is only the quietness of peace as you drift.

I enjoyed being one of the privileged few
Who have died and recovered and brought back the view
Of a Brightness, of Peace, of Contentment and Joy,
Of Memories and Laughter and things that don't cloy.

And yet – in the back of my mind, I recall
As I re-live my life, with the warts and all
Sorts of problems, relationships to solve,
And a new way of thinking for me to evolve.

How can I do it, when I'm set in my ways?
And he who calls the tune usually pays
The full price demanded by the Man made of Rain.
And death shows its hand as we go round again.

'You're dying tonight' said the Man made of Rain,
As my life's story passed before my eyes again.
'You're dying tonight' for the third time he cried
And with that I gave up my life to him, and died –
Yes I did!!!

The Blackbird's Song.(Version 2)

"CAW!" "CAW" "CAW" "CAW"
Crow, Rook, Jackdaw.
Now see what you have done
Gone and lost my Blackbird's song,
To some black bird's guttural sound
For the power of which they are renound!
Crow Rook Jackdaw,
Caw. Caw. Caw. Caw.

Death
(To be read Rythmically).

BeeDomp – BeeDomp – BeeDomp - BeeDomp

A 'Heartbeat' registering a new life,

Baby, teenager, husband or wife.

Family, teacher, grandparents (no strife).

All of life's mysteries pass by the door

One partner dies first, of that you are sure.

A single body, you came to this earth,

For a life's span of years - gave it all it was worth.

And now life is ebbing. Soon under the turf -

BeeDomp - Bee - - Domp - Beeee - - - - D-o—m---p
---- -

Being Alive again!

(Depression Gone!)

Hooray! Hooray! – Oh what a gay day!
An expression you can't use, (or so **P C'**s say).
Life is too short to investigate fully
All repercussions of being a bully.
Sad lives of celebrities – brittle and fraught
With too much of everything, friendships are bought.
So roll on my life-style, easy and pleasant
With friends true and family, round in the Crescent.
I wont change a hair of it, not one iota
'til **'Being Alive'** uses up my life's quota.

Starting with Grace

Lord,
As eagles 'thank you' for the mountains
And fishes 'thank you' for the seas.
May we thank you for ALL our blessings
And for what we shall receive-

Which is not to be like porridge,
Hard to stir and slow to boil.
But to always be like 'Cornflakes!'
Always prepared and ready to serve. Amen.

Anon

Groups and Branches
(Twigs and leaves)

I've been in a group, now, for eight long years and more.
In all that time I've never-HAD-to leave by the 'Back door'!
I started off as Chairman making speeches by the score
And writing little articles, a process I adore.
It wouldn't do for everyone, of that I am quite certain
I'll write this poem just for you, please treat it like the curtain
That on a stage rises and falls, each separate act to contain,
And use it as you will so that your interests you maintain.

Why do I bother, in this verse, to go to this much trouble,
To tell you in these lines, that Parkinson's/uk will double
Both in size of membership, and also finance for research
Now can't you see how it will be, if you're left in the lurch.
You need to know how this disease will treat you in the future
Which research projects we should drop and which we
need to nurture.
It was only research in the brain allowed to be invented
A means of adding wires to it and the problem's circumvented.

Now circumvented means "got round", and by that
means defeated,
And with exercise quite gently done, some standing –
mostly seated,
We socialise, we laugh and joke, we often find it funny
To think that we "Go out to tea," with scones and cream
or honey!
Why shouldn't we? We're just as good as the next man
in the street,
It's just that our legs will not work and we've trouble
with our feet.

But in our group we have the means to discuss each fourth week
The sharing of our problems and to prove that we're unique!

Come and join us and ENJOY.

Philip B. Gibbs
St. Neots 'Group'
Ex-Chair,(Now a 'Twig') on Huntingdonshire 'Branch'.

This piece of verse was written for those people who have been diagnosed, but have never taken up membership of their local group.
What I would like you to draw from this piece , is the fact that although you may not wish to meet other people who are worse off than you, they need your skills and talents to draw them along and make their lives more enjoyable. Strange what a difference a smile makes!

If the above paragraph applies to you, please read the verse again and see if you can change, and try one visit for a start.

P.B.G.

Friday Fellowship

Is there porridge on the menu?
No! There's carrots in the pot.
Betty Camber's famous cooking
Now accounts for quite a lot.

Quite a lot of fellowship
Quite a lot of games
Quite a lot of food consumed.
(I could give you names!)

Names of many 'Fridayers'
For forty years or more
But those who count for everything
Have just walked in the door.

The door is ever open
To all out on the street,
They don't know what they're missing
When the 'Friday Ladies' meet.

What is it holds you all together?
And don't say 'Corsets' – just say whether
It is talking, chatting to the group –
'Hang on girls – Here comes the soup!'

The soup precedes the Main - Course meal
(For forty years its been the deal)
That Betty Cambers Cooks and serves
While Joan Knight sees to the desserts.

The sweets are large, always delicious.
Just once the Lemon Tart was viscious.
'No matter' – (someone thought quite hard),
And Betty 'sweetened' the custard.

Now Betty's custard is the best
I must say. Just forget the rest.
Tastes even better than my mother's.
Can't bring myself to eat 'another's.'

'Fellowship' is mostly food
Which puts the members 'in the mood!'
To play some games, some on their own,
Then off they go. 'Tis time for home.

The 'Social' Club

The Social club's been out to dine.
Some had water, some had wine.
All thought the meal was really fine
Only one thing wrong with mine.

A three course meal I had reserved
With choices taken, and preserved
On waiter's notepad; some hors d'oeuvres,
For me some mushrooms – nicely served.

The main-course came and duly 'went',
No time was lost or even spent
On hacking through tough meat – intent
On value for the money spent.

Everything was nicely done
The meat was fine, the veg. had one
Unusual item known by some
Who said they'd had it at their home.

'Blue cabbage' on Menu today,
And I heard several people say
'I've not seen that before – it's hay
Been coloured, but it tastes OK!'

But now I reach the bit that's hard,
The treacle sponge served with custard
Ran out. In tears I ran into the yard
Hoisted upon my own petard.

Why in tears? Surely you find ideal
The pudding – 'Highlight' of the meal.
It's what I like, it is the deal
For which I came, and now I reel.

Why do I reel? It's just that Hilda
Had the last piece. I can't blame her
She sat down first to choose her dinner,
Told me how good it was, *once it was in her.*

So, I chose something else instead
A 'Stack of Pancakes', same as Ted.
'Tut tut' said his Rosemary, turning red
'So that's what you plan in your shed!'

The moral of the tale is this
Join Ella's Group, to eat in bliss,
The menu's good and if you miss
The thing for which you really wish –

THERE'S A GREAT CHOICE IN MCDONALDS ! !

Octogenarianitis

We have a friend in Ella
And also John her 'Fella'.
They both live life up to the full
And live it by this golden rule;
'Do not do anything to another
That may restrict, or sometimes smother.'
They both pour kindness on the lives
Of those who are friends and then devise
The means to help, advise and listen
With full attention, eyes that glisten,
Who can ask for more than this
From two who seem to live in bliss?

Tho' both set back by movement loss
It seems to matter 'not a toss'.
Young John gets round the house with ease,
You see, he'll roll up both his sleeves
And though confined to his wheelchair
Whene'er we call,- he's always there
To pull our leg, or make a 'dare'.

We like our John, we like his Ella,
We like the family, (should we tell her?)
No – we would only start to babble,
What good would that be - just for Scrabble
Which plays, (with cards) an important role
In keeping brain and body whole.
We do respect you both so much
And recognise the 'Golden' touch
With which you both have blessed our days.
'Happy Eightieth, John', this message says.

Live 'Life' day by day

I am writing a poem for my friend Janet
Who's married to Mervyn, she protects the planet.
She works hard as a carer, does the washing and ironing,
But at times finds the burden, oppressive and tiring.

It's no good telling her, 'We are all the same,'
And 'put aside seriousness, make life a game!'
It's easy to be glib and to make jokes and laughter,
'Be there 24/7', is what 'we' are after.

The carers are special, they just have to be,
They don't have to do it, but it seems to me
That love for a partner could build mountains tall
And accomplish anything, with those warts and all.

The carers are left to their very own devices
They are 'locked' to their partner too long (as in vices).
We expect them to give up their personal being,
But sometimes in their sadness, it's the 'real them' we're
seeing.

It's hard and it's boring and not a part of life
That you chose for yourself, when you became a wife.
You had expectations, for travel and play –
Well 'Keep' them - and 'Do' them - and 'LIVE' day by
day!.

Mervyn's Response.

A poem is coming; it's reaching for air,
This one's for Mervyn, as is only fair.
I wrote one for Janet, bemoaning her fate
Of becoming a carer, tied down just of late.

'I need to do something' I heard Mervyn say,
'Which doesn't take hours, yet fills in my day.
When there are just two of us in this big house,
I stick out like a sore thumb, yet feel anonymous!

It's as if I'm not here, and yet I exist.
I wake in the mornings, then Janet I've kissed
To thank her for bringing me safe through the night
When Demons hallucinate, as if they have the right.

I am not an old man, and yet I have aged
In recent months I've slowed down and then raged
Against what is Parkinson's nasty little game
Of making us all follow and all become the same.

There are, I am told, variations galore
And everyone with it is different for sure.
And yet there's a sameness an inevitable rule
That we will all follow. Some say 'That's cool!'

It is that inevitable outcome that drives
All of us with PD to make something of our lives.
So Janet, just bear in mind, I'm doing my best,
To help out with all the chores, with Fervour and Zest!

I too had designs on retirement's good life
When I'd treat you to everything you want as a wife.
To travel, to sharing in your priority
Now I am frustrated for, it will never be.

Frustration, Frustration that dreaded PD word
That cuts like a knife – NO – more like a sword.
It gets more intense as the years pass away
And I'm forced from life of pure joy – to just day by day.'

But yet I have it in me, to make a go of life,
To put my best foot forward, make you proud to be my
wife.
I'll not let PD dominate and cause us so much pain,
Although it's changed me personally, lets start our life
again.

I'll do the things I used to do, perhaps more slowly now,
We'll give and take a little more, by that means it will
show
We've come to terms with PD's lot, we've put it in its
place,
And though my skill's now limited, the future I will face.

Parkinson's - So What?

I have got Parkinson's, I'm told
Got it while I was growing old.
I never looked as it grew bold
And in my brain it took its hold.

My memory gave out. Its true
That I do not remember you.
Oh! Would I could. And yet I can't.
Because my brain, and thinking aren't......

Able yet to make connection
In between what is 'selection'.
Every brain does this quite rightly,
Parkinson's allows it 'slightly'.

When I realised this was true,
Then I said 'That's enough of you!
My brain will not degenerate
Because I'm in my 'FIGHTING' state!'

Whatever work one undertakes,
You have to realise the stakes
Are so high, you must endeavour
To make sure that you will never......

Let this nasty little microbe
Run your life, through which you just strode.
Do do the things which in your dream
Add to your pride and self-esteem.

It can be done, just look at me
I'm first one up the 'Monkey tree'
I didn't climb that easily
It's far too sharp and prickly.

I did the job, forgot the odds
The tree now lies sawn up in logs.
Proves that, with determination
Things give rise to self elation.

With self appraisal nothing's wrong,
So long as you keep being strong
And work solutions from the heart
Which don't tear all the rest apart.

Keep taking medication, sure
One day someone will find a cure.
'Twil be just like my 'Monkey Tree'
A rude awakening. – Then 'Yippee!!'

Until that day, keep hope alive
By any means. It MUST survive,
Just keep your brain working away,
Amazing things will come to stay!

I know you're frightened now, and yet
We've all gone through it, and I bet
You will come out the other side
With smiles and laughter........and

WITH PRIDE

Where are you going to?

Where are you going to
My 'Special Friend'?
Why are you leaving me
Well before the end?

Our special relationship
Close but not tight
Will hold us together
Night after night.

There is no need to worry
Our friendship's quite secure
We'll meet up, quite regular
Of that I am quite sure.

'Cos I'm back into Parkinson's
I'll do more and more.
Until my brain shuts down
And then shows me the door!

The door to a new life
In heaven or in hell.
The way things are going
It's difficult to tell

Which area of afterlife
Will come out on top!
I'm working t'wards Heaven
I've no time to stop.

There is so much to rectify
This before life goes 'POP'!
And that's what its just done
While you're at the top!

It's those words 'I am leaving!'
Put my mind in a blur.
My heart it stopped its beating
For what seemed an hour.

And then you were weeping
While I stood quietly by,
My mouth could say nothing
Yet my hankie stayed dry,

'Twas not from want of trying
For a tear filled my eye.
May your new job be exciting
And satisfy your need

To give friendship back to all of us
You've done this – Indeed!!.
I just wish you everything
You wish for yourself,

That 'Fame and good Fortune'
Meet up on your shelf.
With a new breed discovered
And named after you,

You never know – with a bit of luck
You may discover two!!

My 'Friend' IAN

I know I knew him long enough
To want to call him 'Friend'
And yes - I knew enough to know
I'd miss him at the end.

Like many, many others
With this damnable complaint,
You end up giving out the vibes
Of something which 'you ain't!'.

I treasure how you looked at me
From under furrowed brow,
And written all across your face
The Question – 'Well? What now?'

I've met a lot of sufferers
From Parkinson's disease,
But only you, in your quiet way,
Would joke and laugh and tease.

I always felt so special
When I came before that look,
And I knew, without doubt, my friend –
You read me like a book!

You never said an awful lot,
Your own counsel you revered
And good advice gave out to those
Who with you, persevered.

I did enjoy those little chats
Of inconsequential merit,
 I am devastated by the fact
You're not going to inherit

All the pent up feelings – which
Develop at the end
Of a very special relationship
Where we call each other -
   'Friend'.

The Sea I See

I stand upon the 'leaward'sided beach
in places where the wind can only reach
in dribs and drabs, and still the sea will roar
as up upon the stones waves break for sure.
'Where have you been?' I call out to a wave.
'I've been to visit Davy Jones's grave.'
With wind behind, the waves grow very high,
so that I'm swept away – perhaps to die.
Not yet, not yet, for I am far from ready
as on my back I float, into an eddy.
Then drop my feet, stand up and feel the bottom.
Thank God for loving me – He'd not forgotten.
Then – the alarm rings, I awake and scratch.
Another dream is done with – there's the catch.

What a reception-ist!

I suddenly feel much better
'cause something's been the matter,
I knew not what
Until I got
The chance to have a natter.

I've had a tooth removed.
My gum had been abused.
Kept me awake
That damned toothache,
'til all my pills I'd used.

So to the Market Square
And to the dentist's there
To get a look
Into the book
Of 'Appointments in the Chair'.

I entered the front door
Walked down the hall, for sure
Who should I see
But my 'Ali'
Returned, and looking pure.

'Where have you been, Young Miss?'
'Come here. Give me a kiss!!'
As she's a sport
Said 'I'm only short –
And can't reach up for this.!'

The desk has built-in height
The kiss, has taken fright.
But with no more ado
On a count of just two,
Young Ali jumped up, took to flight.

She knelt up on top of the desk,
Now, you can guess at the rest.
We had our kiss
'Can't believe I did this!'
She said – adding 'Well I am blessed!'

It just goes to show you how strong
Is the 'friendship of years' and ere long
May it happen to you,
And you find that its true
From one kiss – all your toothache has gone.!!

(I enjoy coming to the surgery!!
I am a Satisfied Client.)

Nothing is 'Simple'

There is a friend I treasure
More than most,
Whose love and wit I measure
More than most
Against the banal attitudes engendered
More than most
By lack of discipline. And
More than most,
The self control required, throughout life.

It takes a special kind of friendship
More than most
To hold on tight to what you feel
More than most
Is that special ingredient.
More than most
Likely to make this friendship shine
More than most;
And cause the friend to be described – 'Divine!'

Divination is the art
More than most,
Of making the ordinary
MORE than most.
How it is done, I cannot,
More than most,
Put into words sufficiently verbose; and
More than 'MOST
DESCRIPTIVE' of my friend.

'Amanda-Jane'.

Amanda – Jane
Made it quite plain
That writing books
Takes more than looks
At grammar and punctuation.

You need a plot.
That takes a lot
Of deep research
From which you lurch
In fear and trepidation.

Research I fear,
Gets nowhere near
Your premise neat
Hero effete
And story near completion.

That's when 'IT' strikes
Your courage hikes
And confidence
Gives way to sense
Of doom and then - cessation.

That's when Ms. A
Just saves the day –
'Write through all that.
I'll eat my hat
If you don't make publication!'

With friends like that
Don't stop to chat
Just write and write
All through the night
Until you make 'COMPLETION'

'My Loss'

My Word! Who is this stranger
Whose mouth has called me 'Dad'?
Why have I no fond memories
Of him, whilst just a lad?

I sit and think in the dead of night,
Demanding brain to work, to right
The obvious trick of non-recall
From which I'm suffering. Explain it all?

I recall when, given the news
That he'd been born, I then refused
To grant him just a little part
Of me, within this hardened heart.

What have you done, you wicked God
To make forgetfulness the rod
By which my life becomes a clod?
Cut off the grass, dig deep the sod.

I sit and think in the dead of night
Of red cap over trousers bright.
A trip to Maidstone, a college room,
Yet he was part of my wife's womb.

'I was good at games', he has just said.
I thought the opposite instead.
'No good at lessons, no academy.'
How come he gained our first degree?

Do you know, I remember not one word
Of conversations overheard?
A lot of whispering with his mother,
And now I know he could do no other.

There was no course that he could take.
I'd cut him off, for heaven's sake!
Now here he is, turned forty two,
I know him better, as do you

As 'Friend' and 'Son' and 'Father' too.
My plea: Your memories review.
Set time aside, if not to pray,
Make time at least once every day

To stop and look and count the cost
Of not remembering, before it's lost.
The sadness of those empty years
Has brought me only streaming tears.

And yet that God, whom I called wicked,
Has seen fit to change my mind
From loose thoughts into something solid,
Because for years I've been so blind.

There's none so blind as will not see,
And that regrettably is me.
Cut off from family and friends,
Tell me – 'What happens if life ends?'

Well – you pass on, full of remorse
Because you've failed to take the course
Which satisfies your human need
To make amends for every deed

Which, like my total cutting off
Caused so much pain. No, don't you scoff,
It's me who now must pay the cost
For everything my boy has lost.

So now my God has been quite fair,
And given me a cross to bear.
A brain disease, with no known cure,
But medication which is pure

And treats the parts which others shun,
And lets me do what should be done
which is, by deeds, to earn forgiveness
and try to live a life that's sinless.

But that's impossible to do,
There's only one of whom that's true.
He was my God's own Son, who came
To reconcile man's life of shame.

I cannot hope to reach those aims
But promise here to meet the claims
On time and love, which put the gloss
On recognizing my true loss.

Palm Sunday

I am the donkey by the fence
An animal supposed to have no sense,
Yet I have all five and plus a sixth-
Why do the people pick up sticks?

Let me tell you about myself,
My mother has left me - on the shelf.
I'm not very big , in fact quite small,
And no-one has ridden me at all.

Then two young men came running by,
 'Disciples of the Lord,' they cry.
'He has need of this young colt,
But are you sure that he won't bolt?'

'I could not swear, ' my master says,
And hands me over with two waves.
One to each of the disciples brave
And I trot on the Lord to save.

To save him from the tragic thought
Which my sixth sense tells me is brought
To the front of his thinking – while he rides
To Jerusalem, there to be denied.

Do you know? They put a rope on me.
Me! Who had always tried strenuously
To buck and kick and kick and bite
Even to braying in the night.

Then He placed a cloth upon my back,
So quiet and gentle was the act.
Then He said, 'Peace be with you – boy.'
And I felt calm and full of joy.

So calm, I could forget the crowds
Of shouting people raising clouds
Of dust and rubbish, which they covered
By laying palm branches cut and lowered.

'Hosanna!' they cried – 'Hail Prince of Light!
Thou God's own Son and our delight.'
And still my sixth sense told me - yet
In just one week they would forget.

The sticks they lay triumphant here
Next week will beat Him, draw a tear.
He, who is so calm and gentle
Will die on a cross, because they're temperamental.

Temperamental in the extreme
And I will witness horrific scenes
And much as I would like to flee
He quietly speaks – 'Peace be!' to me.

And so we reach our journey's end
And I will lose my patient friend
Under a chorus of acclamation
I know He'll be – 'King of every nation'.

My sixth sense tells me this is so,
I know what everyone should know
That, in the face of death and sorrow,
Like Him - go quietly towards tomorrow.

Palm Sunday
(From the donkey's point of view)
Version 2

Hee haw, - Hee haw - Hee Haw - Hee haw.

New Beginning

I drift across the dewy field
With gambolling lambs and ewes, which yield
Their place of safety near the wall,
Where they can shelter – yet see all.

They see the new grass upward growing
And hear the farm cock, loudly crowing.
The cattle call, the chicken cackle
The tractor starts with 'diesel rattle'.

The 'Spring' is here, the sun's warmth tells
Of brighter days and sunny spells
An end to ice, snow, winter pleadings
To make way for our 'New Beginnings'.

'New Beginnings. In every sphere
On life's long journey from there to here.
It is not so long (if looked at quizzically),
Now that Spring has come, quite physically.

(Here will be the beginning of book two.)

Lightning Source UK Ltd.
Milton Keynes UK
UKOW03f2216080814

236618UK00001B/1/P